cross: (verb)
1. to move from one side to another
2. to pass over mediocrity

CROSS THE | LINE®

Copyright © 2017 by Give More Media Inc.
Second edition. All rights reserved.

No part of this book may be reproduced or presented in any form or by any means without advanced written permission from the publisher. Duplication of any part of this book by any form or means is a violation of copyright law.

Cross The Line® is a trademark of Give More Media Inc.
Its logo also should not be reproduced in any way.

Published with love in Richmond, Virginia by
Give More Media Inc. This is the 2nd printing.

ISBN: 978-0-692-80257-1

804-762-4500
InspireYourPeople.com/Cross

CROSS THE LINE®

BY SAM PARKER

CONTENTS

The Line 1

How to Cross It 7

More Thoughts 15

    Choosing to Commit 16

    Working Hard 24

    Focusing 34

    Bouncing Back 42

A Little More on the Big Picture 47

Time to Think 57

With everything, there's a line.

On one side of the line is a greater chance to make good things happen (better results, better relationships, more opportunities). This is where you'll find all those people you admire. On the other side of the line, there's less of a chance.

And with each line, you have a choice.

You want to cross the line or you don't. You want that better chance at making good things happen (meaningful things) or you settle with the lesser chance.

Your choice.

It seems simple but…

Then there'll be those times… those times when in the short run it'll seem like you can't cross the line no matter what you do.

And those misses (those hurdles, those challenges) in the short run will sometimes help you over the line in the long run … in a way you couldn't have seen. They'll serve as lessons … giving you more depth to your experience… making you stronger and better prepared for the bigger and more important challenges you'll face in the future.

But you might not know that at the time.

At the time, you'll just see that line. And it might seem like a wall, but it really is just a line … a line you want to cross.

And it's yours to cross, but you've got to decide (make that **choice**).

It seems simple but…

Then there'll be those people… those people who've decided they'd rather not cross the line and they'd like it if you didn't either. (And, unfortunately, sometimes those people might be your friends.)

Maybe they'll sprinkle in a little doubt or withhold a little encouragement at just the right time … or even encourage you to do the wrong thing. Maybe they'll be a little less subtle about it and just step directly in your way.

And every once in a while, there'll be you … you with that inner voice that'll try to tell you you're not that special and that making something exceptional happen is for other people. (What are you **thinking**?)

Then there'll be the work… the real challenge that some of us never face because of those times, those people, or that inner voice that keeps us from putting in the effort and bouncing back when things get tough.

But there's the line.
And it needs to be crossed.
And **you can** cross it.

It's up to you.

Cross The Line

Which side will you choose?

> "The difficult is what takes a little time; the impossible is what takes a little longer."

Fridtjof Nansen (1861–1930)
Norwegian explorer, Nobel Peace Prize winner

How to Cross The Line...

01

CHOOSE TO COMMIT.

Make that choice to improve your chances to go beyond mediocrity. Approach the things you do with the **intent** to deliver, succeed, and serve.

02

WORK HARD.

Good things are rarely easy (cheap). Real effort and attention are the fundamentals behind everything. There are no quick fixes or silver bullets. Earn your results and push yourself more often than not. That's how you create something special. And, that's what you want.

03

FOCUS.

Eliminate distractions. Minimize your exposure to negative people, thoughts, and things that don't serve your **intent** to succeed. Time moves quickly and you can't get it back. Take good care of it. (You heard that, right?)

04

BOUNCE BACK.

Embrace your challenges. Learn from your mistakes and those of others. Remember your choice to cross the line and make good things happen for yourself and the people around you.

Not always easy … but simple.

ARE YOU READY?

"I have begun everything with the idea that I could succeed, and I never had much patience with the multitudes of people who are always ready to explain why one cannot succeed."

Booker T. Washington (1856–1915)
American educator and civil rights leader

More thoughts…

01 — 02 — 03 — 04
On choosing to commit

Obligated

What if… John and Abigail Adams had been more concerned with themselves and work/life balance than creating a democracy?

What if… Abraham Lincoln had quit trying after his business failed … or after losing his first local legislative race … or after losing a congressional race and two senatorial races?

What if… Martin Luther King didn't have a dream and played it safe (and didn't travel over 6 million miles giving more than 2500 speeches)? What if he thought he was too young to have an impact (he did everything he did in a life of only 39 years)?

What if… Gandhi, Tubman, Mother Teresa, Roosevelt (Teddy, Eleanor, and Franklin), Ford, the Wright brothers, Disney, Gates, Winfrey, Mandela, and Jobs hadn't stepped up and worked hard? (What if the thousands of people who supported them hadn't?)

What if… our police, military, and firefighters didn't? Our parents? Our teachers?

What if… no one pushed it … risked it … and pushed it again (and again)?

Minimize passivity. Be a part of the obligated.
(And stay there.)

> "Let us endeavor so to live that when we come to die even the undertaker will be sorry."

Mark Twain (1835–1910)
American writer

01 — 02 — 03 — 04

On choosing to commit

Better thinking

What you expect to happen … what you believe in your mind … can have a big impact on what actually does happen.

So … if you're going to try to accomplish something… if you make the decision to make the attempt … then the best thing you can do for yourself is to expect a positive outcome. Anything else will only inhibit your efforts.

Worst-case … if you fail, you get an education for your future efforts.

Minimize your doubts and be positively expectant.

01 — 02 — 03 — 04

On choosing to commit

And, remember…

We earn more challenges by dealing with and overcoming more challenges.

Embrace your experience. Enjoy the weather.

> **weathered:** (adjective) seasoned by exposure to the weather
> **seasoned:** (adjective) made fit by experience

"The thing that cowardice fears most **is decision.**"

Søren Kierkegaard (1813–1855)
Danish philosopher

01 — 02 — 03 — 04
On choosing to commit

Boxing it up

Think about your work … your contribution.

Whether you feel lucky or not with what you've been given (or earned) as your opportunity to work, you're ultimately just a steward of it for a relatively brief period in time.

It will be handed off to someone else at some point.

If you thought of that work as being put in a box that will eventually be given to someone else, what would you want the recipient to think when they opened it up?

Wouldn't you want it to be something that's difficult to improve on?

Wouldn't you want them to crack open that box…
look in … smile … and whisper to themselves…
"Wow … that's great work"?

"We would proof our pages like they were going to the Smithsonian. We would check every detail on a set... It doesn't matter if it's a school play or a dumb TV show. It's your work. You should care about it so much that people get annoyed with you."

Tina Fey (1970–)
American writer, producer, and actress

On working hard

Essentiality

"No one's working today," he said to me.

It was a Friday before a holiday that fell on a weekend.

"Some people are," I answered.

"I mean a lot of the people I know aren't."

I asked him where those people worked. He said it was at a local media company.

"How's the news being produced?" I asked.

"Well … some people are working. I was really talking about the nonessentials."

I hadn't heard that phrase in a while. I remember hearing it on big snow days in the Washington, D.C. area when I was growing up … an area with a large number of government employees.

"You don't wish you were nonessential … do you?"

> **essential:** (adjective) of the utmost importance
> **nonessential:** (adjective) not essential

01 — **02** — 03 — 04

On working hard

Here's the thing…

We've all got **168 hours** each week. Sleep 7.5 hours a day and we're left with 115 waking hours.

Invest 40–45 of those waking hours at work and that's 35–40% of our waking life.

That's a big block of time with a choice.

It makes sense to use that time trying to be as essential (valuable, enjoyable) as possible to others. And, it makes sense to lose as few moments as possible to evading that effort.

A more enjoyable day for everyone … that's the goal.

> "Luck is not chance. It's toil. Fortune's expensive smile is earned."

Emily Dickinson (1830–1886)
American poet

01 — **02** — 03 — 04
On working hard

Empty the tank

At the 32nd Annual Kennedy Center Honors in Washington, D.C. (2009), writer and entertainer Jon Stewart described the music icon Bruce Springsteen with…

> Whenever I see Bruce Springsteen do anything, he empties the tank … **every time.** And the beautiful thing about this man is he empties that tank for his family, he empties that tank for his art, he empties that tank for his audience, and he empties it for his country. And we, on the receiving end of that beautiful gift are ourselves rejuvenated, if not redeemed.

Jon Stewart

That "empties the tank … every time" is what gets me.

Most of us don't get the opportunity to empty the tank in such an exciting way as Springsteen, but we can work to empty the tank and be rock stars in our own worlds.

It's just a matter of choosing to hold ourselves to a standard that's not standard at all. It's digging into the details, finding those edges, and pushing a little more … something I call being two-twelve (from my book 212° the extra degree).

You see…

At 211 degrees, water is hot.
At 212 degrees, it boils.
And with boiling water, comes steam.
And with steam, you can power a train.

Just one extra degree makes all the difference.

All kinds of wonderful is waiting for those special people who choose to empty the tank. Will you be one of them?

IF YOU RARELY GIVE A LITTLE MORE, SHOULD YOU REALLY EXPECT TO GET A LITTLE MORE?

01 — **02** — 03 — 04
On working hard

Boring work

I hate doing it.
It stresses me out.
It's so boring.

Every time I hear someone share one of those thoughts, I want to say (and sometimes do), "Who cares?"

I understand and have the same thoughts at times. But I also understand, like so many people that have gone before me, that maybe we're not entitled to everything being perfectly wonderful all the time.

Maybe we need to cuddle up with the fact that just because we don't enjoy every minute of our work doesn't mean we can't be more enjoyable (and valuable) to the people around us.

Maybe we should more often delight in the fact that the opportunity to work (to be of service to others) is a good thing.

Maybe that's our path to a better day.

And one more thought…

All those jobs we sometimes envy (professional athletes, musicians, writers, artists, creative roles, leadership, etc.), they all have their unenjoyable, stressful, and boring components, don't they?

Professional athletes… the drills, the practice, the conditioning, the pounding.

Rock stars… the practice, the travel, the changing tastes of audiences, the redundancy (imagine how excited Bruce Springsteen is about singing Born in the USA … again).

Writers, artists, creatives… the continued need for something new, the dependence on market acceptance, the criticism, the work behind the scenes that's never seen but needed in order to create the things that are seen.

01 — **02** — 03 — 04

On working hard

Leaders… being seen, judged, and held to a higher standard, being responsible for the vision, decisions, and the results (good and bad), persevering and remaining optimistic when things get challenging.

Remember… most of the people who make it to the top of their professions … most dealt (well) with many, many years of difficulty and challenge before they got there. (Weathered and seasoned, right? See page 20.)

"Let's drink to the hard working people. Let's drink to the salt of the earth."

Mick Jagger (1943–)
English music artist

01 — 02 — **03** — 04
On focusing

Distraction diet

Imagine the incredible results you'd have if you focused more during your day.

You'd likely…

- → Contribute more
- → Serve people better (internally and externally)
- → Come up with more ideas
- → Waste less time ramping back up
- → Create more opportunities
- → Plan better
- → Be less frustrated and stressed
- → Help others focus more (by interrupting them less)
- → Make more money (for everyone … including you)

Nothing's guaranteed, of course. But more focus is a better bet to enjoying more.

5 WAYS TO KNOCK OUT THE BULK OF DISTRACTIONS…

1. Establish focus hours for yourself… chunks of time each day where you'll be unavailable to anything but true emergencies.

If you do it with a group of people, commit to no inter-office communications during focus hours unless it truly can't wait. No small talk. No "Hey … real quick" interruptions.

8 am–10 am or 2 pm–4 pm … both blocks of time or whatever fits best for you (and / or your team). When you make a mistake, recommit and remind yourself that more focused time always leads to better results for everyone.

If you're really tough, in order to minimize outside distractions, let your family and friends know your focus hours (and turn off your mobile phone or set it to 'do not disturb'). They'll love you for it … eventually.

01 — 02 — **03** — 04
On focusing

2. Turn off email alerts and commit to checking it at the most minimal level you feel is possible without having a negative impact on service to others.

Most of your inbound emails might be important but likely don't need attention for at least an hour or two (if not longer). Be truthful with yourself and set your interval so everyone wins.

If you can set only two or three specific times a day to respond to email, do it. Consider having an auto-responder that lets people know when you address your email (e.g., "Thanks for your note. I usually check my email three times daily (8:30 am, 11:30 am, 4:30 pm). If you need me immediately, please call my mobile / assistant / office line.").

3. Turn off chat and messaging apps (personal & team) unless your work absolutely requires it to get the job done (key word … absolutely).

Having to phone someone or talk with them live (by visiting them) will make you more aware and respectful of someone else's time (and yours). And everyone's time is important. Be careful with it. Once it's gone, you can't get it back.

4. Avoid the web during your money hours (hours of the workday where you make your good things happen) unless you absolutely need it for your work. The distractions are endlessly wonderful for those who'd prefer to avoid making good things happen (not your goal).

If you must open a browser during your money hours (or focus hours), make sure the opening page is something that doesn't have the potential to encourage you down ~~destruction~~ distraction road (e.g. news or email sites, social networking sites, personal favorites). Search and discover outside your money hours, at lunch, or on a well-earned break.

5. Face away from distraction if you're in a setting that allows you to do so (the door and other people… not those you serve, of course).

Depending on how unfocused you are now, there could be some pain in your efforts to improve. You might fear missing out on something fun or important. You may worry about missing an emergency. But, eventually you'll love where it takes you.

"The major problem of life is learning how to handle the costly interruptions. The door that slams shut, the plan that got sidetracked, the marriage that failed, or that lovely poem that didn't get written because someone knocked on the door."

Martin Luther King, Jr. (1929–1968)
American civil rights leader, Nobel Peace Prize winner

01 — 02 — **03** — 04

On focusing

Money hours

"Rich enough not to waste time."

I've always loved that line. Unfortunately, it was delivered by the bad guy in the movie Wall Street (1987) and mixed in with a little too much 'greed is good' mentality.

But for me, the thought serves as both an inspirational and aspirational reminder to respect and value time … one of the few things in life that once lost, you can't get back.

If you're not earning the income you'd like to earn (or earning the opportunities you feel you should have), ask yourself…

"Am I fully committed? Am I working like someone who makes $X thousand a year? Someone who makes about $Y every money hour of the day?"

Are you valuing your time at that level?

(If not, who will?)

01 — 02 — **03** — 04

On focusing

$50,000 = **$25 every money hour**

$75,000 = **$37 every money hour**

$100,000 = **$50 every money hour** (almost $1 a minute)

$120,000 = **$60 every money hour** ($1 a minute)

$150,000 = **$75 every money hour**

$200,000 = **$100 every money hour**

$250,000 = **$125 every money hour** (over $2 a minute)

More than $250,000…
You probably don't need the reminder.

And today? It's 20% of your workweek. To lose only two workdays a month to fatigue, apathy, or a desire to wait for a better day to do something would be to lose more than a full month* of workdays each year (2 days x 12 months = 24 days). That's scary.

Imagine if your income (and opportunities) reflected your slow days and know that in the long run, it probably does.

---

* Removing weekends and holidays, a month has 19–23 workdays.

"It's work ethic. Over and over and over again, it just comes back to work ethic... How much do you care about your ability to be able to look yourself in the mirror and say 'I worked hard today'?"

Ron Howard (1954–)
American producer, director, and actor
Academy Award winner

01 — 02 — 03 — **04**

On bouncing back

Resilience

> **resilient:** (adjective) capable of bouncing back from or adjusting to challenges and change

We all fail from time to time (our doing, some**one** else's doing, some**thing** else's doing, a combination of each). If we're not failing, we're not pushing it.

To be more resilient…

1. Focus on results. Embrace the fact that results are what we're all really after. Effort and attempts are great first steps, but we need to commit to delivering (just like we want people to do for us).

2. Make lessons of failures. Minimize the tendency to make a failure or mistake anything more than a lesson on how not to do something. We need to learn from our experiences and accept them as tuition for future success. Our mistakes might put us in a bind at times and have some uncomfortable consequences but, that's real life.

3. Continue on. Smarter.

4. Reinforce. Support each other (and ourselves) by continually reminding and encouraging one another to deliver on the first three points.

Be careful not to dismiss that fourth point. It's what makes each of the first three points work.

STAY WITH HOW YOU CAN ... RATHER THAN INDULGING IN WHY YOU CAN'T.

"I attribute my success to this: I never gave or took an excuse."

Florence Nightingale (1820–1910)
English pioneer of modern nursing

01 — 02 — 03 — **04**

On bouncing back

Resignation

Remember...

When things get tough and you occasionally get disappointed that your extra effort, care, and attention aren't giving you an immediate payoff, you can't let that stop you from pushing things.

If you do, then those good habits of working hard, focusing more, and practicing resilience can gradually slip into those bad habits of apathy, resignation, and 'good enough.'

All real progress comes from those wonderful people who keep trying to make things better … regardless of circumstances.

Your 1st question in the face of a challenge … "What can **I do** to make it better?"

"**Nothing splendid has ever been achieved except by** those who dared believe that something inside themselves was superior to circumstance."

Bruce Barton (1886–1967)
American advertising executive
U.S. congressman

A little more on the big picture...

A little more on the big picture

Coachable

You don't know everything. You do know that, don't you?

Other people have gone before you and can help you get to better places faster. But only if you're coachable.

To be coachable is to be…

- → Approachable
- → Attentive
- → Receptive
- → Curious
- → Objective
- → Trusting
- → Grateful
- → Humble

It means you listen with the intent to learn rather than to show what you know.

To be coachable is to lack arrogance and defensiveness… to minimize pride and ego … to let go of the need to be the smartest person in the room.

To be above coaching (development help) is to stagnate or atrophy (waste away) … and in many cases, to be dismissed. To know everything is to be un … believable.

A 6-POINT CHECK ON YOUR COACHABILITY...

Which of the following are true and to what extent? No cute rating scale. Just 6 reflections to help you raise your personal awareness so you can improve things … now. And keep in mind, each of these points work on a personal level too.

1. I regularly ask for thoughts on my work and for ideas on how to improve. (A good thing.)

2. When I'm given feedback / criticism, rather than immediately defending my position, I think for a few moments about the observation shared. (If you don't, how can you give it real consideration?)

3. When I'm given feedback / criticism, I try to better understand it by asking questions on how I can improve. (A good thing.)

4. In the last year, I've changed / revised my position or approach to something because of the advice of someone else. (Is it reasonable to go through an entire year without changing a position or approach to something and still feel you're open to personal development?)

A little more on the big picture

5. I know my work is ultimately about making good things happen for other people. (When you understand that, you're more likely to invite coaching.)

> You're gonna have to serve somebody … yes indeed.
>
> **Bob Dylan**
> American music artist

6. My manager invests time in my professional development. (If s/he doesn't, it might be due to a perception that you're not interested in your professional development and over time, you've been labeled uncoachable … not a good label.)

"You cannot hope to build a better world without improving the individuals. To that end, each of us must work for our own improvement and, at the same time, share a general responsibility for all humanity, our particular duty being to aid those to whom we think we can be most useful."

Marie Curie (1867–1934)
Polish-born French physicist and chemist
Two-time Nobel Prize winner

A little more on the big picture

Evaluation

Do I deliver?
Do others enjoy working with me?

So many details in those two questions. But, if you had to sum up what defines our professional value, I believe that would be it. Forced to make a choice between the two, I'd choose to deliver.

Of course, there's no need to choose between the two. After all, who wants to be a results-producing machine that's tolerated? (Tolerated … ugly word.)

Do I deliver?

Do I make good things happen for other people? Do I exceed expectations from time to time and positively surprise people?

Do others enjoy working with me?

Am I a pleasure to be around? Do I care about others?

Am I patient, kind, and honest? Am I quick to listen (really), slower to speak? Am I encouraging? Am I interested, curious, and enthusiastic? Am I real?

Did I deliver?
Did others enjoy working with me?

Two great questions to put on your calendar for the conclusion of every week … maybe even every day. (Might be helpful personally, too.)

One more thought…

Be sure not to coddle yourself with the answers to those two questions. In the long run, truth will help you enjoy so much more.

> **coddle:** (adjective) to treat yourself in an indulgent or overprotective way

"Be a good ancestor. Stand for something bigger than yourself. Add value to the Earth during your sojourn."

Marian Wright Edelman (1939–)
American activist

A little more on the big picture

Choices

It's what we all really want ... more choices (or put another way ... more control, more autonomy, more freedom).

Because it's much more fun to have more choices on how we live (what we do for our work, where we live, what we eat, what we have) and how we enjoy our time (who we spend time with, where we vacation, what hobbies we take on).

And the best bet to having more choices?

Cross the line and make good things happen for other people.

We do that ... it all works.

CHOOSE TO COMMIT
WORK HARD
FOCUS
BOUNCE BACK

cross: (verb) **1.** to move from one side to another **2.** to pass over mediocrity

CROSS THE | LINE®

Time to think…

Time to think

Where am I good at Crossing The Line?
How can I make sure I stay strong?

Where am I challenged with Crossing The Line?
Why? What's getting in the way?

Thoughts

Time to think

Who do I admire for Crossing The Line?

These are the people I can try to be more like and the people I can recall when things get tough.

Who could I team up with to hold me / ourselves accountable?

It needs to be someone who wants to Cross The Line, tell the truth, and is comfortable with getting uncomfortable.

Who should I minimize (eliminate) contact with?

My time and energy are limited. I need to let go of those who drain it.

Thoughts

Time to think

What unimportant activities are taking away from my efforts to Cross The Line in the important areas of my life?

With what am I wasting time and effort? I can't cross every line, but I need to cross some of them.

What should I allow to have my attention?

Everything has an influence on me … what I read… what I watch … what I listen to. What are the positive influences I'll embrace and the negative influences I'll eliminate?

Am I willing to put in the effort to improve in the areas where I'm challenged?

It might be hard. I might make mistakes. I'll need to be resilient and committed.

Thoughts

Time to think

Where do I absolutely want to Cross The Line?

Top 3 things? If limited to 1, what would it be? Shouldn't I just start there?

By what date will I Cross The Line with my top priority ... regardless of challenges and circumstances?

A specific date will help me hold myself accountable.

Who can / should I help Cross The Line?

With awareness, comes responsibility.

SURROUND YOURSELF WITH GOOD THOUGHTS, GOOD PEOPLE, AND GOOD IDEAS AND MORE GOOD THINGS WILL HAPPEN.

Thoughts

ABOUT THE AUTHOR

I work with a committed team of people in Richmond, Virginia. We create inspiring books, videos, and so much more (find it all at InspireYourPeople.com). We've been at it since 1998.

Our goal is to help people care more about their work and the people they work with and for.

Before co-founding our company, I sold products and services in several different industries (a sales guy).

I'm the author of the bestselling books 212° the extra degree®, Lead Simply™, and Smile & Move®. I write often (see our site below), speak to all sorts of groups and organizations, have a degree in business from James Madison University, and do my best to Cross The Line daily.

Email me at Sam@InspireYourPeople.com. If you're slightly more daring, please call me at (804) 762-4500 ext. 212.

Visit us at **InspireYourPeople.com**.

To all those people who inspire us to Cross The Line... those in our history, those today, and those to come...

THANK YOU.

MORE BY SAM

Most of what I've written is available only at InspireYourPeople.com. All of it can be read in less than 30 minutes (some of it in less than 5 minutes).

While each book/booklet can be enjoyed personally, we've expanded much of the work to include professional development and training material being used by thousands of people at some of the world's largest and best-known organizations. Many of our messages are also very popular within healthcare and education (from K–12 and at the collegiate level).

Our customers have included people at Nike, Gap, Wal-Mart, Verizon, Hershey, Disney, Comcast, the U.S. Olympic Committee, NASCAR, NBC/Universal, NBC/Telemundo, Bank of America, Ernst & Young, New York Life, McDonald's, Tiffany, Target, United Airlines, two branches of the U.S. military, and hundreds of schools, colleges, and healthcare systems.

LEAD [SIMPLY]™

Model. Connect. Involve.

That's your framework for leadership – your simple, day-to-day, in-the-trenches formula for creating that special team of people that does important and meaningful work ... that cares to make things better... continually ... every day.

Model the behavior you want to see.
Connect with the people you lead.
Involve them as much as possible.

That's it. Wonderfully simple.

Lead [simply]™ is a no-fluff, no-parable, no-matrix call to fully embrace (and do) those simple things that can have the biggest impact on making things better.

Learn more and enjoy the 3-minute video at
InspireYourPeople.com/Lead.

212° the extra degree®

212 (two-twelve) is a clear and powerful message that reminds and encourages us to be accountable to the fact that a little extra effort and attention can have a big impact on everything. It begins with the premise...

At 211 degrees, water is hot. At 212 degrees, it boils.
And with boiling water, comes steam.
And with steam, you can power a train.

Just one extra degree makes all the difference.

Learn more and enjoy the 3-minute video at
InspireYourPeople.com/212.

smile & move

This is my follow-up message to 212. It's a reminder to happily serve.

It's all about embracing a positive attitude and taking action.

There are 5 ways to smile (wake up, be thankful, be approachable, complain less, smile more) and 4 ways to move (start early and go long, go beyond expectations, have a sense of urgency, be resourceful and resilient).

Learn more and enjoy the 3-minute video at **InspireYourPeople.com/Smove.**

LOVE YOUR PEOPLE®

We've let too much get between us (each other) and the reasons we're here.

Love Your People is a declaration of care for those we lead and those we serve. It reminds us to be accountable to each other and make good things happen.

There are 8 principles to Loving Your People (contribute, be kind, be patient, be honest, encourage people, apologize, forgive, thank people).

These are the behaviors that will make things better for everyone. It's a 6-minute read.

Learn more and enjoy the 3-minute video at **InspireYourPeople.com/Love.**

"If you learn to respond [to today] as if it were the first day in your life and the very last day, then you will have spent this day very well."

David Steindl-Rast (1926–)
Austrian Monk

Push your luck.
(It's a good thing.)